Saving Birds

HEROES AROUND THE WORLD

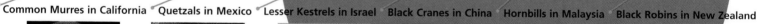

Common Murres in California | Quetzals in Mexico | Lesser Kestrels in Israel | Black Cranes in China | Hornbills in Malaysia | Black Robins in New Zealand

Pete Salmansohn and Stephen W. Kress

Audubon

Tilbury House, Publishers • Gardiner, Maine

Birds are so cool! We human beings just love to see their beautiful colors, listen to their wild sounds, and watch their amazing ways of behaving and surviving. Birds light up our lives with their energy and activity, and help make our days here on planet earth interesting and delightful. But in many parts of the world birds are in trouble.

People have moved into places where birds live and have cut down forests, paved meadows, and drained swamps. People have spilled oil into the seas, shot birds for their feathers and meat, and brought pigs, goats, cats, and rats to wild places where birds nest.

In some unfortunate cases, it is too late to help. Sadly, a number of birds have died out completely and are now extinct. But in places all over the globe, birds and their habitats are being helped by people who care.

The six stories in this book take you to islands and to cloud forests, to cities and to jungles. In these places people are dedicating themselves to making sure falcons and cranes, hornbills and murres, and even the tiny black robin live on and thrive.

The people you are about to meet are true heroes. They work under difficult and sometimes dangerous conditions. They are frequently away from their families and friends for long periods of time. But they roll up their sleeves, do what has to be done, and have faith that their actions will make a difference. In many instances they invent creative and even surprising ways of helping wild birds—successful techniques that no one else has ever tried before.

Join us now for a worldwide journey as we see these inspiring heroes working with patience and dedication to save the world's birds.

Black Robins

Imagine what you'd say if you were asked to save a bird from extinction and there were only five left in the whole world. You might say, "No way, it can't be done." Maybe the word "impossible" would be on your lips.

Not too long ago Don Merton was faced with exactly this challenge. A very cute and perky little bird called the black robin was in deep, deep trouble. It lived on one tiny, windswept island 500 miles off the coast of New Zealand, and if nothing was done to help, it would surely disappear off the face of the earth.

Don Merton is someone whose entire life has been dedicated to protecting birds and wildlife. When he was five years old, he and his brothers found a nest with several goldfinch chicks in it. They decided to put it into the cage of their grandmother's canary, and to their happy surprise the canary quickly took over and raised the chicks as if they were her own.

Don grew up to be a scientist, and in the early 1970s he was asked by the government of New Zealand to go out to the Chatham Islands to see if anything could be done to help the black robin and some of the other species there. Black robins once lived on several of the Chatham Islands, but they began disappearing more than 150 years ago when European settlers arrived and started clearing the forests for farmland.

These settlers had brought many animals with them, such as sheep, cattle, and pigs. They also brought cats and rats. The farm animals destroyed the black robin's forest habitat by eating all the young trees and tramping everywhere. Many birds themselves were killed by the cats and rats. At least seven different kinds of birds were lost forever from the islands. But a few black robins held on at one incredibly small place that animals and people couldn't get to—the Chatham Island called Little Mangere Island.

Old Blue (opposite page) was one of only seven remaining black robins in the world when Don Merton (above) moved them all to the safety of Big Mangere Island. You can see how rough the waters are between Big Mangere Island and Little Mangere, which made getting to the island very difficult.

If you picture an island the shape of a large, fat ice cream cone standing on its head, you'll have some idea of what Little Mangere looks like. It's about 600 feet high, wide at the bottom and small at the top, partly covered by a thin, scraggly forest. To get there you have to ride a boat across an almost always rough and windy ocean, and then use ropes, helmets, and tools to climb steep and dangerous cliffs.

When Don and his team visited in 1972 they counted seventeen black robins and were able to catch and put leg bands on nine. Little did Don know that one of the birds he banded that day with a blue band would go on to be the most important black robin to ever live—Old Blue. Don didn't return to the islands for a while and when he went back to Little Mangere in 1976 the number of black robins had shrunk to seven! Part of the small forest there had been cut away for the construction of a helicopter pad, and the birds were apparently dying off. Don's team from the

From their tiny camp perched on the top of Big Mangere Island, Don and his team watched over the last black robins in the world. Old Blue was the only female left who could still lay eggs, and soon a plan was made to move some of her eggs to other birds' nests. The best foster parents turned out to be Chatham Island tits, but these birds didn't live on Big Mangere. Don and his team had to carry the eggs down the cliff and take them by boat to Southeast Island eight miles away, where the tits lived.

New Zealand Wildlife Service sprang into action and carefully caught and moved the seven birds, including Old Blue, to nearby Big Mangere Island. It was a difficult and terrifying job. Team members had to gently lower themselves over the edge of the 600-foot-high cliff with padded bags on their backs that held the sparrow-sized black robins inside.

Big Mangere Island seemed like a good place to move the birds to because it had a better forest on it, and 120,000 trees had been planted there by the Wildlife Service to improve habitat. But as the scientists watched the birds over the next three breeding seasons, they noticed they weren't doing well at all. In 1979 there were only five robins left, two females and three males. Old Blue and her mate Old Yellow were the only ones that year to successfully raise a chick, since the other pair did not produce fertile eggs.

When the team was getting ready to leave the island for the winter, they saw that Old Yellow seemed crippled and unable to stand. His back toe had somehow slipped inside of his leg band, making it impossible for him to perch on a branch without using his wings and tail for support. After several days of trying to catch him, with the weather getting continually worse, they finally succeeded with a big net, and removed the painful band. Old Yellow flew off, hopefully to survive the winter.

With only five black robins still alive, Don knew something very bold had to be done. But what? Over the years he had noticed that robins can lay more than one group of eggs in a season. Why not remove the first bunch of eggs once they were laid and let another bird incubate them, while the robins laid more eggs? But what other bird would do that, and besides, how would the team move the tiny eggs without damaging them or cooling them off?

A Chatham Island tit feeds a hungry black robin chick. When the chicks were old enough, they were moved out of the tit nests and back to Old Blue, so that they could learn how to be robins.

In 1980, after months of discussion and planning, Don and a couple of other scientists went back to Big Mangere Island. They would take the eggs from Old Blue's nest and put them in the nest of another small bird, the Chatham Island warbler. Meanwhile, they hoped Old Blue, who was already nine years old, would lay more. She was now older than most robins are when they die, so each season she survived seemed like a miracle.

Don's plan soon appeared to be working. Old Blue laid two eggs which were put in a warbler nest. Soon the warblers were incubating the eggs and then feeding the young black robins. Old Blue then laid more eggs. But about ten days later her first chick died! The warblers weren't bringing it the right kind of food.

Don quickly removed Old Blue's second clutch of eggs and took them to the other female black robin—Old Green—and brought the second chick back to Old Blue. Can you imagine her surprise when she came back to her nest and found a big chick instead of two eggs? When the chick saw her it peeped a few times, begging for food. Old Blue immediately flew off, coming back in a few moments with a fat, juicy grub. That summer Old Blue took care of four different chicks, and there were now nine black robins in the world.

Don figured out that the warblers could incubate the eggs but couldn't raise the chicks. What other bird, he wondered, could do the job?

On nearby Southeast Island, which was much bigger than Big Mangere, there was a small brown bird with a yellow chest called a Chatham Island tit. It seemed like a good choice since it built a cup nest like the black robin's and raised its own chicks on insects, like the robins did. But Southeast Island was about eight miles away, which meant a long, cold, wet boat ride while trying to keep the robin eggs warm and safe.

In 1981, each time Old Blue laid eggs Don put them into a strong, warm box he had built, and moved them by boat to Southeast Island. But the big question everyone on the team wondered was whether the tits would accept the new eggs. And would they also feed the young robins once they hatched? Thankfully, the answer was yes—tits made excellent foster parents. And when the robins reached a certain age they were moved out of the tit nests and back to Old Blue, so they could learn how to be robins. At one point in 1981 Old Blue was taking care of five chicks instead of the usual two!

During that nesting season Old Blue, who was still paired up with Old Yellow, laid three different sets of eggs—a truly amazing accomplishment which surprised all the scientists. Old Blue seemed to know that the job of saving the black robins was her responsibility.

For the next six years there was much moving of eggs and chicks from robin nests to tit nests and back again, and from one island to another. Soon there were healthy robin populations on both Mangere and Southeast islands.

When the team returned in 1984 Old Blue was gone. She had died over the winter. But she had raised eleven healthy chicks, and now those birds were having their own families. In 1999 there were 250 black robins, all descended from Old Blue and Old Yellow. What seemed impossible a few years before had now been turned around by the incredible efforts of Don Merton and his fellow scientists. They refused to give up, and with the help of two amazing little birds—Old Blue and Old Yellow—they did something the world is still talking about.

Quetzals   CHIAPAS, MEXICO

Can a puppet show, a song, a coloring book, or a poster help save a bird? If you ask Oswaldo Contreras these questions, he will let out a big laugh and then tell you, "Yes, of course—it is being done right now, here in the mountains of Chiapas, Mexico!"

Oswaldo and his partner Gonzalo Del Carpio can often be found at a school or a meeting, dressed up in a gigantic costume of a very colorful bird called a quetzal (ket–zall). During one of their performances they dance and sing, sharing with the audience why everyone should feel proud of the quetzals. They tell people why there is a great need to help this wonderful bird. "Quetzals live high up in the cloud forests," says Oswaldo, "and they are threatened by people who cut down the trees for wood, and by farmers who set forest fires to clear the land for planting. Grown-ups sometimes shoot them for their feathers, and even young boys with slingshots may try to hit a forest bird."

Oswaldo remembers the very first time he saw one of these blue jay-sized birds, deep in the cloud forest. "It was the most beautiful animal I had ever seen. Its bright green feathers looked like shining metal, and its chest was fiery red. I knew then why Aztec and Mayan Indians looked up to this bird as a God."

Quetzals were indeed worshipped by people of long ago, and their feathers were only worn by kings and other members of the royal family. If an ordinary person was found to have quetzal feathers. he or she would be put to death!

Quetzals live in the moist and cool mountain ranges of southern Mexico and Central America. They eat mostly fruit—especially the aguatillo, which looks like a small avocado. When they cannot find this favorite food, they eat insects, lizards, and small frogs. The male bird is the most colorful and has incredibly long feathers which trail off its back, sometimes as much as two feet or more in length.

A puppet show tells an exciting story that helps people in the cloud forests of Mexico understand why it's important to protect the colorful quetzal, a bird that used to be worshipped by the Aztec and Mayan Indians.

A male quetzal and a chick at the nest hole.

Opposite page: The quetzal needs the forest to survive, so Oswaldo and Gonzalo teach farmers how to grow their crops in the shade of the standing forest, where birds will eat harmful insects and the farmers won't have to use poisonous sprays.

Oswaldo and his partner Gonzalo work for a group whose job is to protect a large park, or reserve, called El Triunfo—the triumph. This area is so rich with animals, plants, and scenery that the United Nations has recognized it as a place that all the world should know about and work to save. It is not, however, a national park like Yellowstone or the Grand Canyon in the United States. It's a part of Mexico where people actually live and work, and many grow coffee beans there, as well as other crops.

"One of the goals we have," says Gonzalo, "is to teach coffee growers that they should not use poisonous sprays on their trees to kill harmful insects. They should grow their coffee naturally, under the shade of the standing forest, to attract birds who will eat the insects. And if they do this, we tell them, they will sell more coffee to people who believe in growing things in a way that also protects the environment."

Gonzalo and Oswaldo are also working to reduce the number of forest fires in the area. "The farmers sometimes set fires," says Oswaldo, "to clear their land. But we show them how to plant their crops without having to clear the forest. It saves the lives of many birds and animals."

These two heroes for the earth get people to pay attention to the problems that El Triunfo Reserve and the quetzal are having in a number of ways, and they quickly discovered that telling an exciting story is something everyone loves. "Our puppets act out a story that begins very peacefully," says Oswaldo, "but soon danger is close by."

The action begins when a quetzal named Rainbow is flying around the trees in his forest looking for food. Soon a mean hunter named "The Exterminator" appears, carrying a gun. But before he can shoot at Rainbow he hears a noise in the bushes and his gun goes off accidentally. An old man with white hair and a white beard then appears. He is dressed in green robes, the same color as the mountains look in the rain.

Dressed in a giant quetzal costume, Gonzalo leads a game with schoolchildren.

He tells the hunter that he is the "Guardian of the Cloud Forest," and he is there to protect the quetzal and other animals. The hunter says he doesn't believe him. Soon the Guardian disappears into the fog, but his voice calls out, reminding the hunter to be respectful.

We then see Rainbow sitting on a branch of a tree. The hunter sees him and fires, hitting Rainbow in the foot. The Guardian quickly comes out of the jungle and is very, very mad. He says to the hunter, "With the power of nature I will punish you and turn you into a fat worm." The hunter laughs and laughs, making fun of the old man.

But in a moment he is changed into a big white worm and becomes very scared. Then the Guardian heals Rainbow's foot.

The next day Rainbow is again flying through the trees looking for food. He spots a worm but he doesn't know it is the hunter. Rainbow flies after the worm, but it hides under the rocks, afraid for its life.

Soon the worm calls out to the Guardian of the Cloud Forest, begging to be turned back into a man. "I am sorry for all the bad things I have done," he says. "I promise to take care of all the quetzals and all the animals that live in the reserve."

The Guardian knows the hunter has learned his lesson so he turns him back into a man and says, "I am giving you a very important job. From now on you will protect the animals and plants in the reserve from hunters, and you will keep people from polluting the rivers and streams."

The hunter is very happy, and he immediately goes over to become friends with Rainbow. From that point on, they watch over the reserve together and keep it safe.

Gonzalo tells children about the quetzal (with the help of Oswaldo in costume), and asks them to help protect the birds.

Gonzalo (left) and Oswaldo (wearing a hat) with a group of proud students who have just written letters to the quetzal, pledging their support.

"This story," says Oswaldo, "touches many people and makes them appreciate the great wonders we have here in Chiapas. After we finish a show we ask the boys in the audience not to fire their slingshots at birds or animals anymore. Some boys even give us their slingshots to keep!" And as a way for everyone to remember Rainbow and the Hunter, the team gives out a book to each student that tells the story and has room for coloring.

More than 20,000 students in 115 schools have seen the performances, and many farmers have heard the message to protect their precious mountains. Gonzalo and Oswaldo have traveled to distant villages, sometimes using mules to carry their puppet theater, coloring books, calendars, badges, and posters. "Wherever we go," says Oswaldo, "people's faces light up with a look that tells us they want to help. Gonzalo and I know then that we are succeeding with our message, and this brings us great, great joy."

Hornbills

SARAWAK, MALAYSIA

The bald eagle is the symbol of America, and a rooster is the national bird in France. But if you travel to Sarawak, a forested land on the Asian side of the Pacific Ocean, you would find a very different-looking bird as the one people honor. The rhinoceros hornbill is big, noisy, and colorful—and has a tremendous beak. It lives in tall trees, eats figs, and has a nest unlike that of any other bird. When the female is ready to sit on her eggs, which she lays inside the hole of a tree, the male makes a sticky plaster of food, rotten wood, and animal droppings and seals her in except for a small hole through which he passes her food! This keeps the female and her eggs safe from predators like snakes. When the eggs hatch and the chicks are ready to come out, the mud wall is chipped away and the whole family begins life together out in the forest.

Hornbills may seem like an unusual national symbol, but they are very important to the native peoples of Sarawak and Malaysia. These tribal

Some traditional dances and ceremonies in Sarawak use hornbill feathers—the dancer in this photo has some real hornbill feathers in his headdress.

15

groups have lived alongside the birds, wildlife, and plants of the lush jungle for thousands of years. They have closely watched the way animals behave, and they have created legends and stories and deeply religious celebrations about the animals. Many of them believe, for example, that hornbills are messengers of God. Carvings and drawings of hornbills are found everywhere, and feathers from their tails are a key part of ceremonies and dances. Long ago only those warriors who had taken a human head in battle were allowed to wear certain hornbill feathers.

It is still popular among many tribesmen to wear hornbill feathers on their hats and capes, and bundles of them are worn around the wrists of women during their dances. The hornbill dance, which imitates some of the interesting ways the bird moves while it is perched on a branch, is especially lovely to watch.

It may not be a surprise then to find out that Sarawak is known throughout the world as

Liz Bennett (opposite page) helped come up with a plan to save the hornbills by suggesting to native people that instead of hunting hornbills, they could use painted turkey feathers or real hornbill feathers from zoos for their dances.

"the land of hornbills." But hornbills are facing many dangers. The forests they live in are being cut down for lumber and wood. Some birds are shot for their meat. And because more and more tourists are willing to pay to see the ceremony of the hornbill dance, birds have been shot just for their feathers. Shocking as it may seem, one hornbill dance group needs 400 tail feathers for the costumes—forty for each of the ten women in the dance group!

If scientists Liz Bennett, Cynthia Chin, and their partners in the Sarawak government hadn't come up with a fantastic and original plan to help save hornbills, these magnificent birds would not have much chance of surviving.

"One day I noticed that the long tail feathers of the hornbill looked a lot like white turkey feathers, except that they had a bold black stripe across them," says Liz. "What about using feathers from turkeys, I thought, and then painting part of them black?"

Liz's idea seemed like a good one, but even if the painted turkey feathers looked like those from a hornbill, would Sarawak's native people accept them?

In the jungle villages of the Orang Ulu people, where many families live together in wooden and reed longhouses, the answer was a surprising yes! "They told us that hornbills are hard to hunt because they perch so high up," says Cynthia. "And that there are so few of them now, they are hard to find." The native people also told Cynthia that if they could get feathers to use for their dances for free, without having to go out and hunt for them, it meant they could do other things with their time, like build canoes or grow crops.

Liz and her team found a turkey farm in Arizona that soon began shipping long white turkey feathers to Sarawak. "Then we needed to find people who could do the painting," says Liz. Women from the Orang Ulu communities were contacted, and it wasn't too long before the

For one dance, turkey feathers are carefully painted and tied in bundles that are attached to the dancers' wrists. For other ceremonies — ones that required the use of real hornbill feathers—zookeepers donated feathers that had been shed by hornbills in American zoos.

women were experimenting with making their own black ink which wouldn't run and smear. They also learned to scrape out part of the feather shaft to make it more flexible and useful for the dance. Groups of the painted feathers were tied together in bundles and then would eventually be put around the wrists of the dancers.

"You really couldn't tell the turkey feathers from the hornbill feathers," says Liz. "Even an expert would be fooled from a distance."

One problem, however, still stood in the way. "There are a few religious ceremonies," says Liz, "which need real hornbill feathers. What could we do?"

Liz thought of her office back in New York at the Bronx Zoo. There, at the international headquarters for the Wildlife Conservation Society, were a few captive hornbills. "We could work with the zookeepers," says Liz, "and ask them to collect feathers shed from their birds. It seemed like a perfect solution."

Liz's fellow scientist Christine Sheppard started talking to zookeepers all across America, and now, she says, "about twelve zoos are sending us their hornbill feathers." The feathers are carefully packaged and are mailed to Sarawak, where the Council on Customs and Traditions loans them out for the special native ceremonies.

Protecting hornbills by using both turkey feathers and zoo feathers is something no one has ever tried before, and it seems to be working very well. But if you go out to the great forests and river valleys of Sarawak you will see that nature itself also has to be protected.

"There is a lot of logging going on," says Liz. "And when loggers build roads into the woods, hunters come, too. The wildlife is disappearing."

Liz and her friends in the Sarawak Forest Department spent ten years traveling through the rugged countryside, talking to people about the problems and what could be done. After much studying they finally came up with a list of helpful ideas, called a wildlife master plan, which they presented to the government. The government agreed with many of their suggestions and new laws were passed to keep unspoiled and wild lands from being logged. It also became illegal for people to sell the meat of wild animals they killed. "This was especially important," says Liz, "because it meant that the forest people who depended on meat would have it, but it kept other hunters from coming in and taking practically everything away."

Loggers who came into the woods to work were told not to hunt, and also not to cut down the big fig trees and hollow nesting trees they came across. By following the rules, they help the hornbills and other animals that still live there have food to eat and a safe place to raise their young.

"Sarawak is the first tropical forest country in the world to have taken these bold steps," says Liz. "Now there is new hope for hornbills and for the forests they live in."

Liz and her group also worked to educate loggers, so that the big trees that hornbills nest in would not be cut down.

Black-Necked Cranes CAOHAI, CHINA

When Li Fengshan, Jeb Barzen, and Jim Harris first traveled to Caohai in the countryside of China more than ten years ago, they could see that nature was in trouble. The rolling hills around the large wetland area were naked and bare—most of the surrounding forests had been cut down. Local farmers were not only digging up precious soil around the edge of the lake to pile up as gardening areas, but they were also pulling up wild plants to feed to their animals. If all this human activity continued, the thousands of cranes, geese, ducks, and other birds that depended on this "sea of grass" would leave.

What was truly amazing to these scientists was that Caohai was an official Chinese nature preserve! "It looked like a moonscape," says Jeb. "And where there were once about 400 black-necked cranes using the marshes, now their numbers were less than 300."

For thousands of years Caohai had been a rich home to birds and wildlife. But as the population of China grew, and as the governments changed, large projects to help rural people were created. In 1958 orders were given to drain the lake so that farmers could have more land on which to grow their crops. But the draining did not quite succeed. In 1972 another attempt was made and this time the giant lake was finally gone. All that was left of the water was a little stream and some wet areas. It soon became clear to many people living in the area that the government's plans were creating a nature nightmare. The new land was either too dry or too wet. Winds blew down from the nearby mountains, bringing nasty dust storms. And insect pests attacked their crops.

In 1982 a decision was made to restore the lake. A dam was built and water started covering up the croplands. But now the farmers were furious. The land they had learned to depend upon was now being taken away and they were in danger of not having enough food. The birds suffered, too, because the hungry farmers were pulling up marsh plants for their pigs—plants the birds would have

Black-necked cranes need Caohai's wetlands for their winter feeding grounds, but over the years the lake and most of the marshes had been drained to provide land for poor farmers. If the wetlands were restored, would the farmers still have enough land to grow their crops?

Jim Harris meets with farmers, trying to find a solution that will help the birds and the farmers both.

liked to eat themselves. Some birds were shot or trapped for their meat.

A few fights broke out between the farmers and the managers of the preserve, whom the farmers blamed for their problems. "There was always a tension in the air," says Li Fengshan. No one, it seemed, was winning. Not the people and not the birds—especially not the graceful and endangered black-necked cranes that needed Caohai for their wintering grounds.

In 1994 Fengshan, Jeb Barzen, and Jim Harris from Wisconsin's International Crane Foundation teamed up with Chinese officials and others to try to save both Caohai's birds and the poor farmers who lived there.

"We all had something in common," says Jeb. "We all agreed that cranes were important and we didn't want to lose them."

In Asia cranes are symbols of long life and happiness. Pictures and statues of cranes are found every-

The farmers used to harvest wetland plants to feed their animals, but now they work on projects like this new birdwatching tower, to bring tourists to the area.

where, and people are fascinated by their great beauty, their size, and their interesting behaviors and sounds. Black-necked cranes stand almost four feet tall and are considered mysterious because they nest in faraway places, high up in the mountains. In the late summer of the year they leave their nesting grounds in the cold and windy marshes of the Tibetan Plateau and fly to Caohai and a few other choice wetlands where they spend the winter.

After months of discussion with the still untrusting villagers, a plan was finally drawn up. Small gifts of one hundred dollars would be given to farmers and families to help them start businesses or learn skills, as long as those businesses did not harm the Caohai nature preserve. Zhang Xicai bought tools so he could make money as a carpenter. Miao Xiangian bought supplies so she could make tofu, to be sold at the town market.

Villagers also used money provided by the nature reserve to improve life for everyone who lived there. People bought trees to plant on the hillsides

Everyone needs to have a good job. These two women work with their husbands to repair bicycles and radios. These small businesses are funded by the project and have made a big difference in the lives of local people.

where they had been cut down. Drinking wells were fixed up, electric lines were built into some areas, and money was used for kids to go to school and for teachers to be hired.

At the village of Bojiwan, very close to the lake, townspeople patrolled the shoreline to keep fishermen's boats and people's farm animals away from the waterbirds and the places they needed to nest. They repaired roads and built platforms alongside Caohai Lake so tourists could see cranes and other marsh birds. As word got out around China that things were improving at the wetland, more and more birdwatchers and tourists started arriving every year.

"The farmers and the nature reserve managers have now become partners," says Jim Harris. "They are no longer enemies."

A second part of the plan involves teams of American volunteers, some of whom come to Caohai to study and observe the birds. "We need to know what the cranes eat and where they go," says volunteer leader Jim Rogers. "The more we know, the better we can protect them and their habitats." Other volunteers go into schools to help students and teachers build pride for the cranes. "We brought them pictures of cranes done by kids in America," says Jim. "By showing them that people from the outside think their cranes are beautiful and important, we help them appreciate what's here in their own backyards."

In so many different situations the farmers, villagers, and young people of Caohai have opened their hearts and minds to new ways of doing things. They have seen very clearly that their lives are bound together with the cranes and wildlife that call this exciting wetland their home. "Environmental problems and people problems can be healed at the same time," says Jeb Barzen. "Caohai is proof of that."

The project has also helped provide new desks and books at the village school, livestock such as pigs for local farmers to raise and sell, and basic tools for a variety of small businesses, such as the one above where men are making stoves out of used oil barrels.

Lesser Kestrels

ISRAEL

It's eight o'clock in the morning on a summer day in the ancient city of Jerusalem, and the phone is ringing at Ifat Schulman's desk. A young boy is on the line. He is very excited and is almost crying, and at first Ifat has a hard time understanding what's wrong. A young falcon has fallen to the street, he tells her. It's outside his house, and he is scared that it will get run over. Can she come right away?

Ifat rushes out to her car and drives quickly through the narrow streets between the old stone buildings of Jerusalem to the address the boy has given her. The boy and his family are out on the road to meet her, and soon they are all peering under a parked car to where the bird is hiding. Ifat sits down on the pavement and shimmies herself under the car. Thirty seconds go by and nothing happens. Then Ifat slowly backs out holding a fuzzy little falcon, known here in Israel as a lesser kestrel. By this time most of the neighbors have gathered and everyone is trying to get a close look at the most famous bird in Jerusalem—an animal they've been told is among the earth's threatened species.

Lesser kestrels have only recently become bird movie stars in Israel, thanks to the work that Ifat and other scientists from the Israel Ornithological Center are doing. And it's a good thing, too, because without a lot of attention the lesser kestrels could disappear. In the 1950s there were about 5,000 pairs nesting in Israel, but now there are only about 550 pairs. They can also be found in parts of North Africa, Europe, and Asia, but they are in trouble there, too.

Kestrels are falcons—fast-flying birds that catch and eat living things like crickets or mice or even other birds. Falcons have a thick hooked beak that they use for tearing flesh. And because they are such keen hunters, people trap them to keep as unusual pets, or to sell. There are six kinds of falcons nesting in Israel, and many of them need help to survive.

"There are lots of reasons why the lesser kestrel has been having problems," says Ifat. "They eat insects, and in many places farmers are poisoning insects. Also, farmland and open space is lost every year to

These birds are looking for a place to call home. Lesser kestrels often use tiles and drainpipes on the tops of buildings as places to put their nests.

27

Israeli and Palestinian students look for some of the lesser kestrels that nest near this desert town.

make new towns and villages, and the birds have fewer places to hunt for food. Here in Jerusalem some of the old houses are being replaced by modern apartment buildings, and that means the tile rooftops and drainpipes kestrels like to nest in are gone."

It's only been about six years since the work to save lesser kestrels began, but Israeli scientists have quickly come up with an amazing variety of ways to help. "Our neighbors in Jerusalem watch over the fifty or sixty nests that are scattered around the city," says Ifat. "And they use the 'hotline' to call

us when something happens. We've also worked out a deal with a large wine company to make special bottles of wine with the bird's picture on the label. And we've created an exciting program for kids that is now being used in twenty schools— ten in Israel and ten in the U.S."

Students can quickly jump right into the middle of the lesser kestrel's life by logging on to an Internet site to see all the action in an active nest. Thanks to a camera that is mounted nearby, people have a chance to watch a mother bird feeding its chicks or a dad flying in to take over. Some students have

been lucky enough to go out to the desert to see a large kestrel colony—a place where many nests are side by side.

Here they learn that lesser kestrels do things that many other birds of prey do not do—they nest in colonies and they hunt in small groups. This kind of behavior helps them in many ways, including protection from predators, and not having to search for food alone. By grouping together, they help each other survive.

Scientists watching kestrels in the cities began noticing that when adult birds went out to hunt they would often fly as far as six or seven miles for just one cricket. Michal Frankel, an American biologist who works with Ifat, says that because it is so hard for the adults to find insects in an area filled with houses and buildings, many of the their nestlings were starving to death. In the city, she says, "the adult lays about five eggs but only one or two chicks survive. In the country, where there are grassy areas for the kestrels to hunt in, four or five chicks will make it"

When a lesser kestrel spreads its wings, they measure about two feet from tip to tip.

As Michal looks on, Ifat holds an antenna in hopes of tracking a lesser kestrel fitted with a radio transmitter.

In 2001 the team created a new project to help change this sad situation. They now remove several eggs from the city birds' nests and take them to a zoo to be incubated. But they are also careful to leave two eggs in the city nest, because they know the adults there can raise two chicks.

When the removed eggs hatch in the zoo, the chicks are fed for about three weeks. "Then we take them to two places in northern Israel," says Ifat, "where there is a rich food supply." Bands are put on their legs and after a while they are set free. Since the project began only recently, it is too early to tell if these particular birds will return to northern Israel when they come back in spring from their wintering grounds in Africa. "We are anxiously waiting for the coming year to see who returns," says Ifat.

The hopes and dreams of Ifat, Michal, and others who work so hard for lesser kestrels sometimes collide with things they never imagined. In the Middle East that means fighting and violence between Israelis and Arabs. It was only a few years ago that Arab students from Palestinian neighborhoods started working with Israeli children to build wooden nest boxes for the kestrels. At the time of their first meetings there was a feeling of hope among the adults and students. Dan Alon, who runs the Israel Ornithological Center, and Palestinian Nader Al Khateeb had teamed up to bring children together whose people have had a long history of war and mistrust. Maybe, they thought, the kids will learn to get along because they would all be working on one goal—to help the kestrels.

Building that cooperation and trust took time and energy, and things seemed to be going well. The students built more than a hundred kestrel nesting boxes. Then, war broke out between the Israelis and Palestinians. There has been violence, and there has been death. And, unfortunately, there has been an end to the students working together.

Michal Frankel has also watched the fighting interfere with her studies and research. "I need to follow the birds to see where they are going for food," she says, "but soldiers sometimes stop me now."

Ifat and Michal very much hope that Israelis and Palestinians can live peacefully with each other. In the meantime, the work goes on. Scientists will again be following the kestrels once they fly back to Israel this March. Birds will be weighed, measured, and banded. Some will have radio transmitters attached to them. More eggs will be incubated at the zoo, and more chicks released. And the Jerusalem neighbors will watch the nearby nests to see if any chicks fall out. But in order to really succeed with helping the kestrels, the team knows that people from different backgrounds need to get along, too.

"When human beings learn to live together," says Ifat, "it will be a good day for wildlife."

Israeli and Palestinian students built more than a hundred nesting boxes together. In the photo above, two male kestrels are competing for this nesting box, while below, four lesser kestrel chicks look out of their own nesting box.

Common Murres

DEVIL'S SLIDE ROCK, CALIFORNIA

High cliffs are easy to reach if you're a bird. But for scientists who wanted to put bird decoys on top of Devil's Slide Rock, getting there was a scary and dangerous job. First they had to leap out of a wave-tossed boat onto the slippery rocks. Then, using strong ropes and special safety equipment, they had to slowly and carefully climb the wet and slimy cliff walls.

Excitement like this is probably not what you think of when you imagine people trying to save birds. But for a team of young scientists hoping to give the common murre (pronounced "murr") a new start on the California coast, there were many heart-pounding moments. "Murres nest in places where predators and human beings can't get to them," says biologist Mike Parker, "so we had to figure out ways to do the impossible."

To some people, even the idea of bringing back a colony of lost seabirds sounded like a fantasy. In the early 1980s more than 1,400 pairs of murres had nested on Devil's Slide Rock. Then, in 1986,

Getting equipment on and off Devil's Side Rock is no small challenge!

a barge carrying oil was caught in a storm and one of its hatch doors broke open, spilling thick gooey oil into the ocean. As the 20,000 gallons of oil spread out, it covered birds, seals, and other animals. Eventually about 10,000 seabirds died, including about 6,000 murres.

Murres were also dying along the California coast because of another reason. Fisherman's gill nets, which are set out like a long nylon curtain in the sea, are supposed to catch fish. Unfortunately, they also catch murres, puffins, and other diving birds that drown if they get tangled up in the net.

So the murres, who are cousins to the puffin, were disappearing along the central coast of California. What could be done to help them?

After years of battles in the courts, the oil company responsible for the spill was forced to pay the government approximately five million dollars so an attempt could be made to restore, or bring murres back to Devil's Slide Rock. The United States

Fish and Wildlife Service was asked to do the job, and they called on Steve Kress, a famous ornithologist who had succeeded in restoring puffins and other seabirds to several islands in Maine. Steve was very enthusiastic about this new challenge and traveled to California to help assemble a team and create a plan.

One of the team members was Susan Schubel, who had worked with Steve on the Maine seacoast. Her first trip out to Devil's Slide Rock was hair-raising. "There were enormous ocean swells about ten feet high," she says. "I had to keep looking at the waves, watching the seas as I got ready to jump out of the boat. The first time I tried it, I fell in!"

In the late winter of 1996, Susan, Mike, Elizabeth McClaren, and others began the awesome job of bringing 400 wooden murre decoys, two sound systems, solar panels, batteries, and twelve large mirror boxes up to the top of the 150-foot-high Devil's Slide Rock. They also carried powerful tools to drill holes in the rock where the decoys would

stand. It took three full days to set everything up, and then the waiting began. "After that point, it was up to the murres," says Elizabeth. If the murres saw the decoys and mirrors and heard the recordings, they might think there were other murres on the rock and build their nests there again.

Each day team members drove to a tiny dirt parking lot at the edge of a gigantic cliff overlooking the ocean and Devil's Slide Rock. They set up high-powered telescopes and looked through them, out over the quarter-mile distance to where the decoys were placed. "We could hear the murre sounds coming from the CD players we set up out there," says Sue, "and with all those decoys it looked just like a real murre colony."

On just the second day of watching, amazingly enough, two real murres were seen. "They were chasing each other around and looking in the mirrors," says Sue. "We were very excited—it happened so fast!"

Sue trims material from a murre chick decoy, while Elizabeth places adult decoys at the very top of Devil's Slide Rock. The decoys, along with mirror boxes and recordings, are used to trick murres into thinking that there are already other murres iving on Devil's Slide Rock.

A few more murres arrived as the days went on, but no one believed they'd see nesting pairs that first year. "We figured we'd be lucky to have murres nesting within about ten years," says Steve Kress. "They raise just one chick at a time, and the birds don't breed until they're about four or five years old, so it takes years to restore a seabird colony like this one."

Sue and her teammates were excited when they starting seeing what they called "pair behavior" or "pair bonding."

"The male and female would walk together, and take turns arranging each other's feathers," says Sue. "Sometimes they would stand up really straight and tall, parading together like penguins. We also saw them mating."

Several long chilly months of watching and waiting went by, and about a dozen murres had shown up. "We started getting suspicious whenever a bird sat in one spot for a long time," says Elizabeth. "We wondered if it was sitting on an egg." Then one day she saw a murre stand up—and underneath it was a pointy greenish egg. "I started yelling, 'An egg, an egg!'" says Elizabeth. "It was the most beautiful egg I'd ever seen."

That was May 26, a great and memorable day for all those on the project. Five more eggs were eventually laid, for a total of six active nests. For the first time in history murres had been lured back to a place where they once nested—proof that people can indeed start new seabird colonies. But no one had yet seen what is the most spectacular moment in a young murre's life—when the flight-less chick jumps off the cliff where it is born, down into the ocean, to begin life as a seabird.

Since it takes about thirty-one days for a murre egg to hatch and another twenty-one days for the chick to be strong enough to leave (or "fledge"), team members were on the edge of their seats during early July. "We kept peering through the telescopes, wanting to be the first person to see that chick jump off the rock," says Susan.

On July 12 they saw a large chick walking around the top of the cliffs, a behavior they thought would surely lead to the great leap. But when they came back the next day, hoping to see it again, the chick was gone and so were its parents. "We were disappointed," says Mike, "but it was still a great feeling to know our idea was working, and that

Elizabeth looks out to Devil's Slide Rock from the mainland, hoping to see real murres and their chicks among the decoys.

one chick had successfully fledged." The young murre would spend the next few months of its life with its father, learning to fish and survive on the open ocean. This first chick was a promise of hope for the future of Devil's Slide Rock—hope that if it survived sharks and oil spills and gill nets, maybe it would come back to nest.

Two more chicks fledged that year, much to the delight of other scientists in California who had known about the project and were watching for results. Every year since then, more murres have returned to Devil's Slide Rock, and more chicks have hatched. During the breeding season of 2001, a record 110 pairs of murres raised chicks.

"I think of the terrifying times we had to jump out of the boat and then climb those cliffs," says Sue. "And then there were all those long days we spent watching and waiting from the parking lot in the cold and dampness. But when we saw those chicks—wow! We really did it—the murres did come back!"

THE AUDUBON MISSION IS TO CONSERVE AND RESTORE NATURAL ECOSYSTEMS, FOCUSING ON BIRDS, OTHER WILDLIFE, AND THEIR HABITATS FOR THE BENEFIT OF HUMANITY AND THE EARTH'S BIOLOGICAL DIVERSITY.

Through its education, science, and public policy initiatives, Audubon engages people throughout the U.S. and Latin America in conservation. Audubon's Centers, and its sanctuaries and education programs, are developing the next generation of conservation leaders by providing opportunities for families, students, teachers, and others to learn about and enjoy the natural world. The science program is focused on connecting people with nature through projects like Audubon at Home and the Great Backyard Bird Count. Audubon's volunteer Citizen Scientists participate in research and conservation action in a variety of ways, from monitoring bird populations and restoring critical wildlife habitat to implementing healthy habitat practices in their own backyards. Audubon's public policy programs are supported by a strong foundation of science, environmental education, and grassroots engagement. Working with a network of state offices, chapters, and volunteers, Audubon works to protect and restore our natural heritage.

To learn how you can support Audubon, call us at (800) 274–4201, visit our website at http://www.audubon.org, or write to Audubon, 700 Broadway, New York, NY 10003.

RESOURCES FOR MORE ABOUT THE BIRDS AND THEIR HEROES:

Giving Back to the Earth: A Teacher's Guide to Project Puffin and Other Seabird Studies
by Pete Salmansohn and Stephen W. Kress
Paperback, $9.95; ISBN 0-88448-172-7
8-1/2 x 11, 80 pages, illustrations
Grades 3–6

"Educationally sound, it offers a wide variety of experiences to enhance and enrich the student's understanding of puffins, seabirds, and the oceans. ...This is a marvelous and fun resource."
—*Appraisal*

Here are more than 40 creative, hands-on activities: art projects, role-playing, wildlife observations, science demonstrations, running games, and more. The guide is organized into seven major themes, including seabird adaptations, the marine ecosystem, human impact on the environment, people making a difference for wildlife, and more. Includes annotated bibliographies and Internet resources. Available from Tilbury House, or through your local bookstore. Approved for the California Supplemental Materials Fund, and on the New York City Textbook List.

Black Robins in New Zealand
Department of Conservation
P.O. Box 12416
Wellington
New Zealand
www.doc.govt.nz/

Quetzals in Mexico
Rare Center for Tropical Conservation
1840 Wilson Blvd., Suite 402
Arlington, VA. 22201-3000
www.rarecenter.org

Hornbills in Sarawak
Wildlife Conservation Society
2300 Southern Blvd.
Bronx, NY 10460
(718) 220-5100
www.wcs.org

Black-Necked Cranes in China
International Crane Foundation
P.O. Box 447
Baraboo, WI 53913
(608) 356–9462
www.savingcranes.org

Lesser Kestrels in Israel
Israel Ornithological Center
P.O. Box 58020
Kiriat Atidim
Tel Aviv
Israel 61380
www.birds.org.il

American Society for the Protection of Nature in Israel
28 Arrandale Avenue
Great Neck, NY 11204
(718) 398–6750
www.teva.org.il/e/

Murres in California
United States Fish and Wildlife Service
P.O. Box 524
Newark, CA 94560
(510) 792-0222
www.desfbay.fws.gov/murre.html

The Audubon Seabird Restoration Program
159 Sapsucker Woods Road
Ithaca, NY 14850
(607) 257-7308
www.projectpuffin.org
This program has also been very successful restoring puffin colonies on islands off the coast of Maine, a story featured in *Project Puffin: How We Brought Puffins Back to Egg Rock,* by Steve Kress and Pete Salmansohn. You can help continue Audubon's Project Puffin by adopting your own puffin. Each $100 gift will enroll you in the Adopt-A-Puffin program and assign one Atlantic Puffin to you. You will receive your puffin's life story, a full-color photograph of your puffin, and a certificate of adoption. Many classes and schools have raised money through bake sales, bottle drives, and other methods to adopt a puffin. For more information, visit the web site above or write to Project Puffin, Audubon Society, 159 Sapsucker Woods Road, Ithaca, NY 14850.

TILBURY HOUSE, PUBLISHERS
2 Mechanic Street, Gardiner, ME 04345
800–582–1899 • www.tilburyhouse.com

AUDUBON
700 Broadway, New York, NY 10003
212–979–3000 • www.audubon.org

DEDICATION — To all the recognized and unrecognized heroes whose hard work and dedication are helping to save the earth's biodiversity.

ACKNOWLEDGMENTS — The creation of this book, over a period of almost two years, is the result of the generous and ongoing help of many people. We would first like to thank all the "heroes" and "heroines" who are featured in the text: Don Merton, Mike Parker, Susan Schubel, Elizabeth McClaren, Ifat Shulman, Michal Frankel, Dan Alon, Nader Al Khateeb, Oswaldo Contreras, Gonzalo Del Carpio, Jim Harris, Jeb Barzen, Li Fengshan, Jim Rogers, Liz Bennett, Christine Sheppard, and Cynthia Chin. We also want to thank Cynthia Koenig, Rafael Manzanero, and Beth Trask of the Rare Center for Tropical Conservation; Alejandro Grajal, Debbie Wood, Rose Borzik, Clare Tully, Frank Gill, and Sandy Clough of the National Audubon Society; Kate Fitzwilliams and Susan Finn of the International Crane Foundation; Yossi Leshem of the International Center for Bird Migration and Robin Gordon of the American Society for the Protection of Nature in Israel; Diane Shapiro and Tom Veltre of the Wildlife Conservation Society; and Jayl Langub of the Sarawak Council of Customs and Traditions. We would also like to especially thank Jennifer Elliott Bunting, Tilbury House's publisher, for her continuing commitment to this book.

PHOTO CREDITS — *Black Robins:* Don Merton: 2, 3 (l), 4, 5, 6, 7 (r); Rob Campbell: 3 (rt); Nigel Miller: 7 (rt). *Quetzals:* VIREO: 8; Rafael Manzanero: 9 (t), 16 (l), 12 (m), 13 (r); M. and P. Fogden: 9 (r); RARE: 10, 12 (t & b), 13 (l) Aaron Ramirez Velozquez: 11 (l). *Hornbills:* Wildlife Conservation Society: 14, 18, 19 (b); Doug Wechsler: 15, 19 (t); Morton Stampe, WCS: 16 (l); Tom Veltre, WCS: 16 (r); Bill Meng, WCS: 17. *Black-Necked Cranes:* International Crane Foundation: all. *Lesser Kestrels:* Society for the Preservation of Nature in Israel: 26, 27, 28, 31; Hanne and Jens Erikson, VIREO: 29; Courtesy of Michal Frankel: 30. *Common Murres:* Steve Kress: 32 (r), 33 (r), 34 (l), 37; U. S. Fish and Wildlife: 32 (l), 33 (l), 34 (r), 35, 36.

Library of Congress Cataloging-in-Publication
Salmansohn, Pete, 1947–
      Savings birds : heroes around the world / Pete Salmansohn, Stephen W. Kress.
          p. cm.
Summary: Profiles adults and children working in six habitats around the world to save wild birds, some of which are on the brink of extinction.
      ISBN 0-88448-237-5 (hc : alk paper)
      1. Birds, Protection of--Anecdotes--Juvenile literature. [1. Birds--Protection. 2, Wildlife conservation. 3. Endangered species.] I. Kress, Stephen W. II. Title.
      QL676.5 .S23 2002
      333.95'816--dc21
                                   2002006720

Designed by Geraldine Millham, Westport, MA.
Editorial and production work by Jennifer Bunting, Audrey Maynard, and Barbara Diamond.
Color scans by Integrated Composition Systems, Spokane, WA.
Printing and binding by Worzalla Publishing, Stevens Point, WI.